SPORTS ALL-STARS
ALEX OVECHKIN

Anthony K. Hewson

Lerner Publications ◆ Minneapolis

SCORE BIG with sports fans, reluctant readers, and report writers!

Lerner Sports is a database of high-interest biographies profiling notable sports superstars. Packed with fascinating facts, these bios explore the backgrounds, career-defining moments, and everyday lives of popular athletes. Lerner Sports is perfect for young readers developing research skills or looking for exciting sports content.

LERNER SPORTS FEATURES:
- Keyword search
- Topic navigation menus
- Fast facts
- Related bio suggestions to encourage more reading
- Admin view of reader statistics
- Fresh content updated regularly

and more!

Visit LernerSports.com for a free trial!

Copyright © 2020 by Lerner Publishing Group, Inc.

All rights reserved. International copyright secured. No part of this book may be reproduced, stored in a retrieval system, or transmitted in any form or by any means—electronic, mechanical, photocopying, recording, or otherwise—without the prior written permission of Lerner Publishing Group, Inc., except for the inclusion of brief quotations in an acknowledged review.

Lerner Publications Company
A division of Lerner Publishing Group, Inc.
241 First Avenue North
Minneapolis, MN 55401 USA

For reading levels and more information, look up this title at www.lernerbooks.com.

Main body text set in Albany Std.
Typeface provided by Agfa.

Library of Congress Cataloging-in-Publication Data
Names: Hewson, Anthony K., author.
Title: Alex Ovechkin / By Anthony K. Hewson.
Description: Minneapolis : Lerner Publications, [2020] | Series: Sports all-stars | Includes bibliographical references and index. | Audience: Age 7–11. | Audience: K to Grade 3.
Identifiers: LCCN 2018052616 (print) | LCCN 2018055345 (ebook) | ISBN 9781541556201 (eb pdf) | ISBN 9781541556102 (lb : alk. paper) | ISBN 9781541574472 (pb : alk. paper)
Subjects: LCSH: Ovechkin, Alexander, 1985-—Juvenile literature. | Hockey players—Russia (Federation)—Biography—Juvenile literature. | Hockey players—United States—Biography—Juvenile literature. | Washington Capitals (Hockey team)—Juvenile literature.
Classification: LCC GV848.5.O94 (ebook) | LCC GV848.5.O94 H48 2020 (print) | DDC 796.962092 [B] —dc23

LC record available at https://lccn.loc.gov/2018052616

Manufactured in the United States of America
1-CG-7/15/19

CONTENTS

Raising the Cup 4

Facts-at-a-Glance 5

An Early Star 8

Staying Strong 12

A Hero Off the Ice 16

The Capitals' Captain 22

All-Star Stats 28

Source Notes 29

RAISING THE CUP

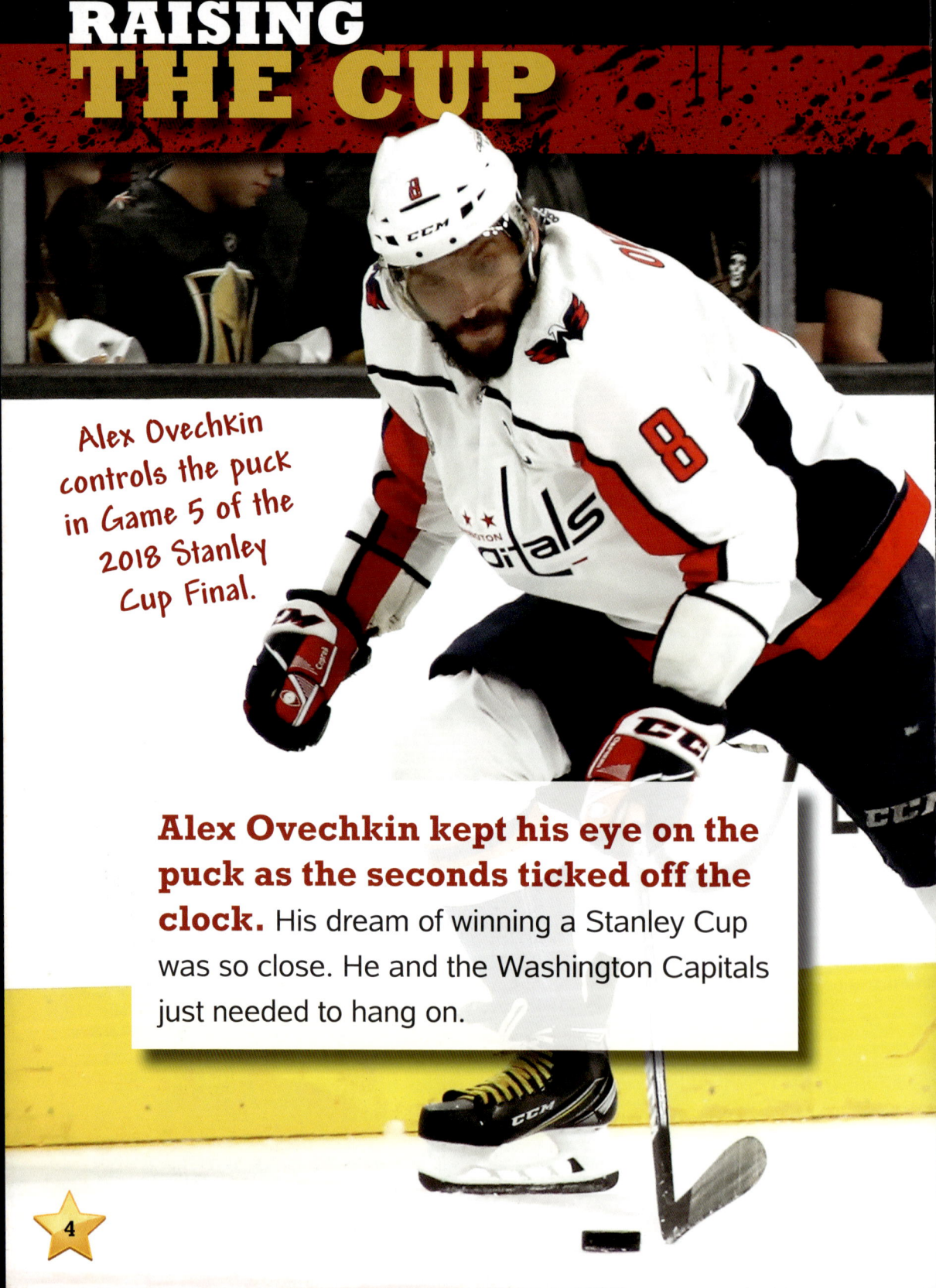

Alex Ovechkin controls the puck in Game 5 of the 2018 Stanley Cup Final.

Alex Ovechkin kept his eye on the puck as the seconds ticked off the clock. His dream of winning a Stanley Cup was so close. He and the Washington Capitals just needed to hang on.

- **Date of Birth:** September 17, 1985

- **Position:** forward

- **League:** National Hockey League (NHL)

- **Professional Highlights:** drafted first overall by the Washington Capitals in 2004; 2006 NHL Rookie of the Year; three-time NHL Most Valuable Player (MVP); 2018 Stanley Cup champion

- **Personal Highlights:** son of a pro basketball player mother and pro soccer player father; married in 2016 and had his first child in 2018; does **charity** work in Russia and the United States

In 2009, Ovechkin won the Hart Memorial Trophy, which is given to the NHL MVP.

For 13 seasons in the NHL, Ovechkin worked to bring a championship to Washington. He was a three-time NHL MVP. He was one of the greatest goal scorers of all time. He was a fan favorite. But Ovechkin felt his career would not be complete without winning the Stanley Cup.

During the 2017–2018 regular season, Ovechkin scored the most goals of any NHL player. In the **playoffs**, he took it to another level. His strong playing carried the Capitals to the Stanley Cup Final.

Ovechkin scored two goals as the Caps won three of the first four games in the championship series. If they won Game 5, they'd win the Stanley Cup.

Game 5 went back and forth. Ovechkin scored his team's second goal of the game. With two minutes left, the Caps were clinging to a 4–3 lead. The Vegas Golden Knights pulled their goalie. This gave them an extra

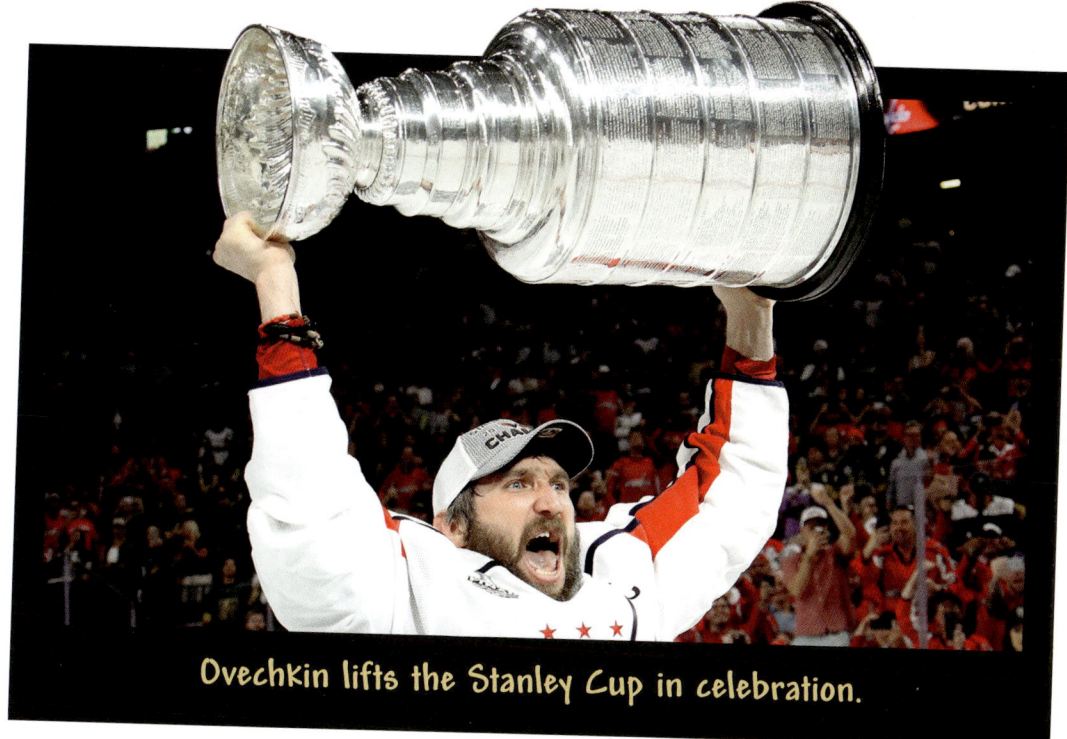

Ovechkin lifts the Stanley Cup in celebration.

skater on the ice. They were trying to score a goal to tie the game.

But the Capitals never gave them a chance. Ovechkin watched as the game neared its end. He knew his team was going to win.

As the clock ran out, Ovechkin leaped into the air. He yelled and celebrated with his teammates. He lifted the Stanley Cup above his head. He was a Stanley Cup champion.

"This moment, I'll remember for the rest of my life," he said. "I'm so happy. It's unbelievable."

AN EARLY STAR

Russians of all ages are hockey fans.

It is no surprise that Alex Ovechkin grew up loving hockey. The sport is very popular in Russia, where Alex was born. But there were early signs that Alex loved hockey more than most.

When he was two years old, Alex saw a toy hockey stick in a store. He grabbed it and refused to let go. At age five, he saw a hockey game on TV while his dad was flipping through channels. Alex cried until his father changed the station back to hockey.

Alex started playing hockey when he was seven. He came from an athletic family. His mother won two Olympic gold medals in basketball.

Alex's parents were both very involved in sports while he was growing up.

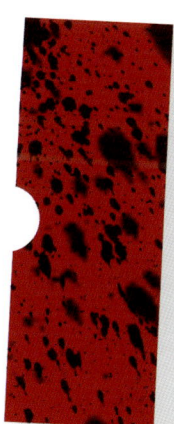

Tatyana Ovechkina, Alex's mom, was voted the best female point guard of the 1900s by readers of a Russian sports newspaper.

His father played soccer. His older brother Sergei was a wrestler.

In Russia, seven years old was a late start for a hockey player. But once Alex chose hockey, his family encouraged him, especially Sergei. Alex looked up to his older brother.

When Alex was 10, Sergei was in a car accident. He died after the crash. Alex was devastated. But the next day, he played in a hockey game. He felt that's what his brother would have wanted.

"I was on the bench, I was crying," he recalled. But he still played. Sergei's death inspired Alex to work even harder at hockey.

For high school, Alex went to the hockey academy Dynamo Moscow. Unlike public school, the academy let Alex focus on hockey. Alex woke up at 6:00 a.m. each day

Alex poses for a photo with students at Dynamo Moscow after winning the Stanley Cup.

to eat breakfast. Then he went to hockey practice. He had two hockey practices each day at school. Then when he got home, he played more hockey.

"You dive into sport with your head and arms and legs, and there's no time for anything else," he said.

By age 16, Alex was playing in Russia's top professional league. His size and skating ability caught the attention of NHL teams. The Washington Capitals selected him as the first player in the 2004 NHL Draft.

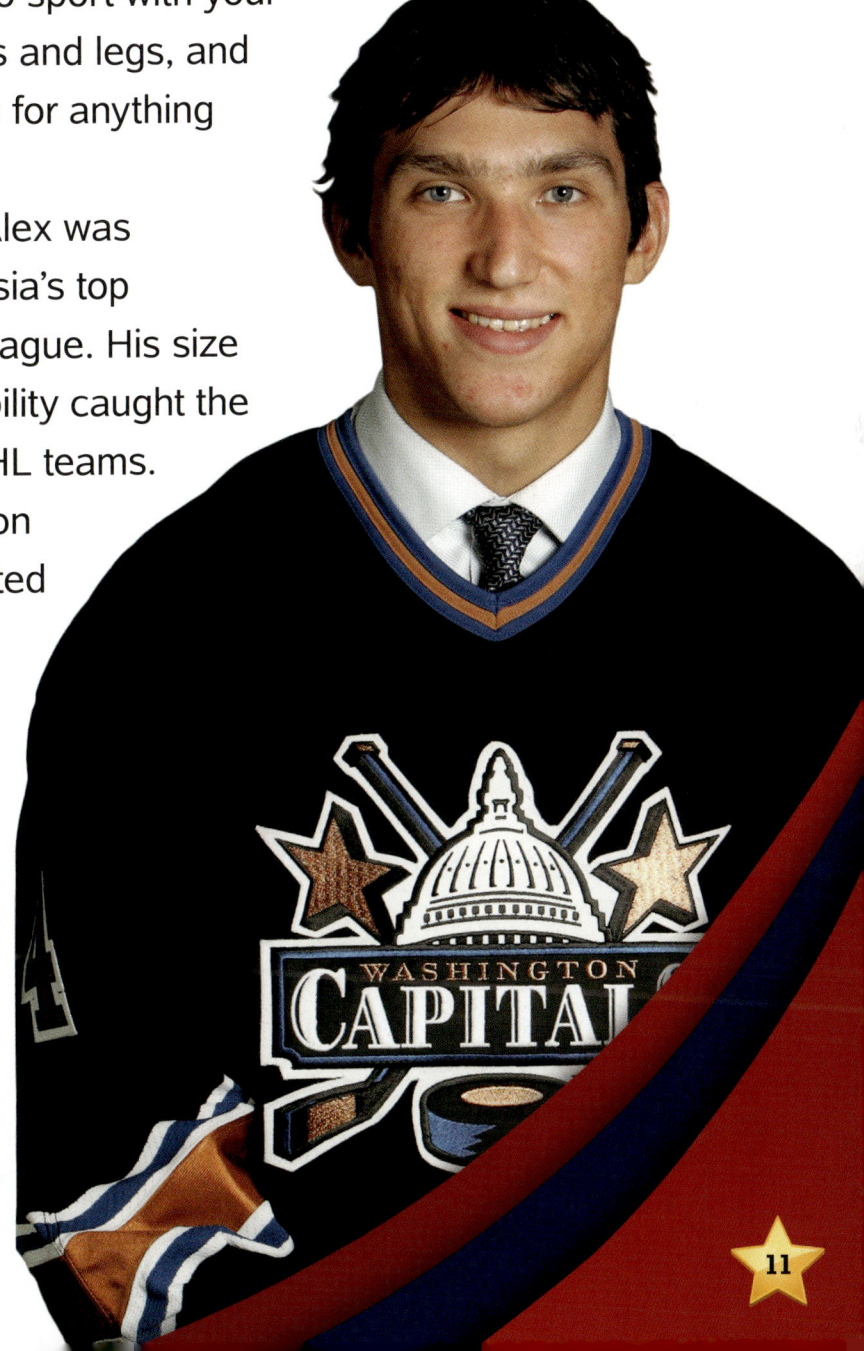

Alex wears a Washington Capitals jersey after being chosen as the first NHL Draft pick in 2004.

STAYING STRONG

Ovechkin focuses on the play during a game against the Vegas Golden Knights.

At six foot three (1.9 m) and 235 pounds (107 kg), Ovechkin has a presence on the ice. He has the strength and size to beat just about anyone to the puck. But Ovechkin's game is about more than just power.

Ovechkin spends a lot of time training and staying active so he can be a great hockey player.

In the gym, Ovechkin works on his **endurance**. A hockey season lasts 82 games, plus the playoffs. Ovechkin needs to make sure his body is ready for the long season.

The **off-season** is an important time to stay in shape and train. During the off-season, Ovechkin runs about two miles (3.2 km) per day.

Squats are a big part of Ovechkin's weight training. He regularly hires a strength coach and **personal trainer** to help him stay on track throughout the year.

Strength helps Ovechkin with shooting. Ovechkin's **slap shot** can top 100 miles (161 km) per hour. At that speed, a goalie barely has any time to try to stop the shot.

At the 2018 NHL All-Star Skills Competition, Ovechkin won the title for the hardest shot. His slap shot traveled at 101.3 miles (163 km) per hour.

If Ovechkin gets within 25 feet (8 m) of the net, his shot is too fast for a goalie to stop. The goalie just has to hope he has enough of the net covered. If Ovechkin picks the right spot, he's going to score.

Ovechkin takes a shot.

But Ovechkin takes most of his shots as wrist shots, or wristers. With a wrister, the puck does not move as fast as it does with a slap shot. But wristers can be more on target. To shoot a wrister, Ovechkin keeps the puck on his stick while picking a place to shoot. With a flick of his wrists, Ovechkin shoots the puck fast. Sometimes he will fake the shot first to throw off the goalie.

Ovechkin works on his strength and skills all the time. But the mental part of the game is also important. Ovechkin works to stay focused. But he also has **superstitions**. During the Capitals' Stanley Cup run in 2018, Ovechkin did not want to leave anything to chance. He started each practice the same way, taking a lap around the rink first before the rest of the team joined him. He did all media interviews from the same spot in the arena. He even made sure there was a stool in the same place each time.

As he enters the later stages of his career, Ovechkin has to keep working hard. He won the Stanley Cup, but his hockey career isn't over yet.

Ovechkin prepares to warm up before a game.

A HERO OFF THE ICE

Ovechkin plays for Team Russia in the 2016 World Cup of Hockey.

Ovechkin is hugely popular in his home country of Russia. He is treated like a national hero. Not only do fans like watching him succeed in the NHL, but he has been a star of the Russian national team since he was a teenager. He led Russia to gold medals at the World Championships in 2008, 2012, and 2014.

Ovechkin plays in a 2016 charity basketball game to raise money to help children with cerebral palsy.

But Ovechkin is a hero for more than what he's done on the ice. Ovechkin helps many people in Russia and in his US home of Washington, D.C. He has given money to help Russian **orphanages**. He has worked with the Make-a-Wish Foundation to help make the dreams of sick children come true. He has held charity games too.

Ovechkin poses for a photo with a fan.

Ovechkin is also known for his random acts of kindness. In October 2017 the Capitals were in Edmonton, Canada, to play the Oilers. Ovechkin was shopping with teammates and spotted a homeless man wearing no shirt in the cold weather. Ovechkin bought the man a coat, sweater, and hat. If a reporter had not recognized Ovechkin, nobody would have ever known about his good deed.

Ovechkin supports his home country's national soccer team.

Ovechkin and Nastya Shubskaya pose outside of a theater in 2017.

Ovechkin's fun-loving personality also makes him a fan favorite. After the Capitals won the Stanley Cup, Ovechkin was seen celebrating all over Washington. He and his Caps teammates brought the trophy everywhere they went, taking pictures with fans and letting them experience the fun.

"Now we can celebrate all together and remember this moment for all our lives," Ovechkin wrote on social media after winning the Stanley Cup. "Time to party Caps fans!!!!"

In 2016 Ovechkin married his girlfriend, model Nastya Shubskaya. Just minutes after winning the Stanley Cup in 2018, Ovechkin announced that they were expecting a baby. Their son, Sergei, was born that August. Sergei was named after Ovechkin's brother.

THE CAPITALS' CAPTAIN

Ovechkin (left) celebrates with a teammate after scoring a goal in his first NHL game.

Ovechkin poses with the four individual trophies he won in 2008.

Ovechkin burst onto the NHL scene just weeks after his 20th birthday. In October 2005, he played his first game with the Capitals. He scored two goals in that game and hasn't looked back.

Ovechkin scores a lot of fantastic goals. In January 2006, Ovechkin scored a goal against the Phoenix

Coyotes while sliding on his back after a fall. Hockey journalist Bill Clement called it one of the greatest goals of all time. Ovechkin led all rookies that year in goals and total points.

By 2008, the Capitals had made Ovechkin the focus of their team. He signed a 13-year **contract** that year. After the season, he won a trophy as the NHL's MVP.

Ovechkin won four major trophies again in 2018. This time, the Stanley Cup was one of them.

Ovechkin led the league in goals, scoring 65. That earned him another trophy. He won another trophy after being voted the league's best player by the other players and a fourth trophy for leading the league in combined goals and assists. Ovechkin was the first player to win all four trophies in one year.

Ovechkin celebrates after scoring a goal.

Ovechkin led the league in goals scored again the next year. In 2010 the Capitals named him team captain. Ovechkin was racking up goals and honors. But one award he didn't have was a Stanley Cup. The Capitals were a good team. They usually made the playoffs, but they never got very far.

Everything came together for the Caps during the 2017–2018 season. Ovechkin was back on top of the league in goals scored with 49. The Capitals had their best season ever, finally winning their first Stanley Cup. Ovechkin was named MVP of the playoffs.

In early 2019 Ovechkin ranked number 15 in all-time goals scored with 639. He still had a long way to go to catch Wayne Gretzky's record of 894. But at age 33, Ovechkin was as strong as ever on the ice. Someday he might top Gretzky's record. But whether or not he breaks the all-time scoring record, Ovechkin will be remembered as one of the best scorers in NHL history.

Ovechkin controls the puck during a game in 2018.

Number of Games to Reach 500 Goals

575 Wayne Gretzky, 1986
605 Mario Lemieux, 1995
647 Mike Bossy, 1986
693 Brett Hull, 1996
801 Alex Ovechkin, 2016
803 Phil Esposito, 1974
833 Jari Kurri, 1992
861 Bobby Hull, 1970
863 Maurice Richard, 1957
887 Marcel Dionne, 1982

Source Notes

7. Greg Beacham, "At Long Last, Ovechkin and Capitals are Stanley Cup Champs," *CBC Sports*, June 8, 2018, https://www.cbc.ca/sports/hockey/nhl/stanley-cup-vegas-golden-knights-washington-capitals-game-5-1.4696954

10. "Alex Ovechkin Opens Up for First Time about Brother's Death," *Fox Sports*, October 9, 2015, https://www.foxsports.com/nhl/story/washington-capitals-alex-ovechkin-opens-up-about-brother-s-death-100915

11. Michael Idov, "Ovechkin With Love," *GQ*, October 24, 2010, https://www.gq.com/story/alexander-ovechkin-nhl-washington-capitals

21. Cindy Boren, Scott Allen, Sarah Larimer, Ava Wallace, Michael E. Ruane, Rick Maese, Jacob Bogage, and Faiz Siddiqui, "Capitals' Stanley Cup parade: Ovechkin's Speech Brings the Celebration to a Wild End," *Washington Post*, June 12, 2018, https://www.washingtonpost.com/news/capitals-insider/wp/2018/06/12/capitals-stanley-cup-victory-parade/?utm_term=.88549cd25bd8

Glossary

charity: an organization that helps other people or raises money for a good cause

contract: an agreement for a player to play for a certain team

endurance: the ability to do something difficult for a long time

off-season: the time of year when a sports league is not playing

orphanages: group homes for children who do not have parents

personal trainer: a professional who works with a person to help them exercise and stay fit

playoffs: a series of games after the regular season that determine which team wins the championship

slap shot: a powerful shot in which the player swings the stick at the puck

superstitions: beliefs that unrelated actions or routines can affect the outcome of an event, such as sports game

Further Information

Alex Ovechkin Career Stats
https://www.hockey-reference.com/players/o/ovechal01.html

Alex Ovechkin Olympic Bio
https://www.olympic.org/alexander-ovechkin

Alex Ovechkin Washington Capitals Bio
https://www.nhl.com/player/alex-ovechkin-8471214

Kortemeier, Todd. *Alexander Ovechkin*. Lake Elmo, MN: Focus Readers, 2019.

Savage, Jeff. *Hockey Super Stats*. Minneapolis: Lerner Publications, 2018.

Washington Capitals. New York: AV2 by Weigl, 2015.

Index

charity, 5, 17

Dynamo Moscow, 10–11, 19

Most Valuable Player (MVP), 5, 6, 24, 26

National Hockey League (NHL) Draft, 11

off-season, 13

Ovechkin, Sergei, 10, 21

Russia, 5, 8, 9, 10–11, 16–17, 19

shooting, 13–15

Stanley Cup, 4, 5, 6–7, 15, 19, 21, 25–26

superstitions, 15

Washington Capitals, 4, 5, 6–7, 11, 15, 18, 19, 21, 23–26

weight training, 13

World Championships, 16

World Cup, 19

Photo Acknowledgments

The images in this book are used with the permission of: © Bruce Bennett/Getty Images Sport/Getty Images, pp. 4–5, 7, 24; © Ethan Miller/NHL/Getty Images Sport/Getty Images, p. 6; © Donat Sorokin/TASS/Getty Images, p. 8; © Mary Gelman/The Washington Post/Getty Images, p. 9; © Vladimir Gerdo/TASS/Getty Images, p. 10; © Scott Halleran/Getty Images Sport/Getty Images, p. 11; © Dave Sandford/NHLI/National Hockey Leauge/Getty Images, p. 12; © Patrick McDermott/NHLI/National Hockey League/Getty Images, pp. 13, 15, 27; © Jonathan Kozub/NHLI/National Hockey League/Getty Images, p. 14; © Dave Sandford/World Cup of Hockey/Getty Images, p. 16; © Artyom Korotayev/TASS/Getty Images, pp. 17, 19; © Andre Ringuette/NHLI/National Hockey League/Getty Images, p. 18; © Brian Babineau/NHLI/National Hockey League/Getty Images, p. 20; © George Bridges/MCT/Tribune News Service/Getty Images, p. 22; © Steve Russell/Toronto Star/Getty Images, p. 23; © Roy K. Miller/Icon Sportswire/Getty Images, p. 25.

Front Cover: © Patrick Smith/Getty Images Sport/Getty Images.